Sis Fuss

Sis Fuss
Nikia Chaney

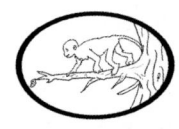

Orange Monkey Publishing, 2013

© 2013 by Nikia Chaney

ISBN-13: 978-0-615-75237-2
All rights reserved.
Printed in the United States of America

Published by Orange Monkey Publishing
22797 Wren St.
Grand Terrace, CA 92313

www.orangemonkeypublishing.com

Cover art by Christine Coates
http://ccpainter.com

Contents

Sis Fuss Is Born	1
Sis Fuss Smarting Up	2
Checking in with Sis Fuss	3
Sis Fuss Speaks	4
A Wifey for Sis Fuss	5
Sis Fuss Best Friend	6
Sis Fuss Turning Off the TV	7
Sis Fuss Saves the World	8
Bedded Sis Fuss	9
Sis Fuss Weeps	10
Sis Fuss Phone Call #3	11
Sis Fuss Listening	12
Pushing Sis Fuss	13
Sis Fuss P.O.ed	14
The White Rock and Sis Fuss	15
Sister and Sis Fuss	16
Sis Fuss Stringed	17
Syllogizing Sis Fuss	18
Sis Fuss Goes Home	19
Sis Fuss Locked Back Up	20
Sis Fuss Epilogued	21

Sis Fuss Is Born

Sis knew that
he should not
have been able to fit
on the futon. Sis was
a giant in the room. Sis sat
on tiny futon touched tiny
fridge tiny little table
phone book chair. Sis
had wide hands. Hands that could hold
the weight of his body fit in the space
of the breath make
sense cut up air.
If he knew why
only those hands
worked why the heat shimmered mirroring the white
rock on the plush green carpet and why he could not
speak he thought that he might be something
not bulky or vast but
fit thick neat.

Sis Fuss Smarting Up

   Sis Fuss liked to dress. He liked
the pants going up and way the shirt
ironed warm rode slow on his chest.
   Made him feel like a woman
     was touching
him using him to rest her messy
   head. Sis liked to look good to wear
     black hats to step outside in hard
pointing shoes shined cloth cut
   in square shapes that defined
     a big bodied man. A
       nigga in a suit Sis
       might say leering
        at the mirror because
       even though the silk felt
     good it would not stop
    his fingers from snagging
on the four tight strings as he turned
     and turned and turned and flexed.

Checking in with Sis Fuss

The lady behind
the glass had fingernails
painted black
on every other
tip her toes
were apparently
partially made in France too.
She slide her finger across
her phone screen one
more time and looked
up and looked
up at Sis Fuss who looked down
at the curtain of her
bangs razored sharp at the left
eyelash sitting thick
at the calculation
calculus maybe
the odds of him
getting anything other than a key.

Sis Fuss Speaks

You ain't
right Fuss.
How you
going to ride
17 miles
everyday
to the dump. How
the fuck you
going make it
with a flat tire
a broken chain
no pump. Shut
up and think. Shut up
and get
your pimple butt
together. You got a
week in this
motel. No more no less. Sit up, Fuss.
Ask. Speak.

A Wifey for Sis Fuss

An asymmetrical walk.
    A broken tooth.
  A large bottom lip.
Long hair in
    a poof style that Sis Fuss
 knew he would want
    to touch.
 A scent of dove or
 maybe dial soap.
 Pretty little tiny feet.
She didn't have to be too much.
If Sis could found
    a reflection of himself
    in window of her car get
 a slow thick look
 lessen the pull of just
      a one damn string
    plant his own smell on her sheets
well then.

Sis Fuss Best Friend

                Cigarettes can be
            legal tender in certain
                  circles that is
            unless they are
wet. And five years ago a man
                  shit even three
                    could get
              into a program a
              hustle a woman's
              sweet sweet bet a
                path towards some
          fool's necessary dream.
                      But 53,
            fifty three, fif -
          tee three even the sound
                  of it soaked
                through and
          Sis lighting up knew that
              nobody would let that.

Sis Fuss Turning Off TV

Motel used to say two things. Cable and TV.
Or was it Cable and Phone. Or maybe
just HBO. No that was later but definitely

before the W I F I

sign that always made Sis
wonder what in the hell did wifi
stand for and why in this motel room was it so damn necessary.

Maybe now everyone had slide

phones and laptops
and intranet cords connected to the smart

chips leaking out the back sides of their brains
beepers on they asses anything

not peopled

to talk or touch
and hold on to a body a real wifi wifey. So he held tight
the remote in the hand

point and shoot black plastic
and hard

easy no instructions needed.

Sis Fuss Saves the World

On tv there was this show
about the dead rising up
and taking over the world.

Sis Fuss watched with only
a slight frown
because the little girl

zombie was kind of cool bloody
mouth and makeup and all.

He liked too the empty streets
the way the paper blowed

all around the small
breezes that showed it really was fucked up
the meat and meal of the story.

He put himself
and his white
rock and his four
trembling strings for a just while

smiling in the background among
the quiet streets and fake screams.

Bedded Sis Fuss

All these women
ain't shit. Whiny
ass tiny little pieces
of nothing. Nothing.
Not one god
damn thing.
And we just run tail
behind them
like some
kind of damn dogs
or dolls looking
for place and peace. Yeah
pieces of shit
women
just caring about the cash. Then
he scratched his rock
and watched the curve of her back
as she put
on her dress.

Sis Fuss Weeps

Sis Fuss did not cry like a baby
  or a woman or even an old man.
     He did not make noise. His body
       did not shake. Sis just
        doubled
         over and purged the contents
    of his belly. He folded down
   on his stone
    his head caught up
     in the puppet wire
    his toes pointed toward the bubbling
   foul smelling green carpet stream.
 And when the phone
rang out like a siren
 wailing for acknowledge panic access
    Sis turned and reached
     past the bed for that piece of black
    plastic as if it were
 a sweet potent drink.

Sis Fuss Phone Call # 3

Hey man, yeah,   been out five days, huh.

A truck? You'd have to pick
    me up.
        In Chino? Nah I can't, p.o.

    A job?   Hauling what?

Scrap metal ain't what it used to be.
Shut up!   You said that.   A job?

Doing what?   Huh.   Go 'head. How's your brother?
He still with that girl?   No the other one.
    Yeah. It's all fucked up.

No not the back,

the front.   That's what he get.
    Sister.
She good. Called me yesterday.

Three kids. Two girls and a boy.

    Yeah, fucking bike.   It's flat. No, not that my .22.
I need to come get it.   Shit. Okay, I be there later.
    Take care, man.   You, too,
        good luck.

Sis Fuss Listening

"Where are you Siseal?
Just tell me
where you are?"
    Sis waited.
"I can come to you,
I can get you,
you can come here..."
    Sis sighed.
"Will you talk to me?
Siseal,
Please."
Sis hung up the phone.
      Well she
    sounded
    good at
    least she
    sounded like
      she was
        happy.

Pushing Sis Fuss

Like some kind of Jack
Lalane. Like six
packs and being
cut shoulder

            belly butt

hard as that
damn white rock.

            Like a man
should be rough
hands feet hunger
gleen. Like eating hot
bacon in bed. Like the suck
of a pipe weaponed and steam
and sliding

          round in luck
cold and wet.

          100 200 4.
Like being a young man again
summed and dumb.

Sis Fuss POed

Never trust a man
named James.

Smiling dancing lying wire
rimmed frames and pink
mouth with the tendency to drip
shit in those lips big like
some kind of pompus fucking pig.

Of course I've got
a place to go. My sister said
she'd take me in and
no I'm done with drinking
and please and thank you

yes sir I will be here tomorrow to
kiss your ass some more cause
you are god almighty and you
know exactly what I am
with your greasy hands gripping
my goddamn
strings.

The White Rock and Sis Fuss

        Like yellow
pebbles surrounded
by skin

and a grin was worse.
   Like sand grating
              the flesh
under the lip
     or a load
          under hand
to be bit to be pulled pushed.
   Like leaning
            on the floor

wet and cold. Like
     losing time space
    the why. And maybe the

   blood and gristle
          tastes good
and the purpose of a gun
           completes.

Sister and Sis Fuss

See the thing about sisters younger
or old was that
in the end they'd be
women. And Sis could only remember

the girl pretty little
and proud ready

to follow him all around every goddamn
room. His sister
might disagree. She
might say that Sis was mean too

busy to reach down and pick up
a barbie doll's lost
shoe make funny a scary
dream. She might say that

Sis was cold and
empty and sold only on his own

things so how could he ask for a quiet
space in her house
full of happy people frills whistles family.

Sis Fuss Stringed

Sis had four strings
riding out the small of his

back. The strings were
slack and made

out of piano
wire reeled out slag

metal things that pulled him to

and fro. Sis would pick up
an arm and the high

left side string would
twang and yank

his wrist slick
through the air. But Sis did not care

too much that

he could not choose his moves.
It was the quiet here

that cut him
and the waiting for the moment at hand

the bat the stroke a way back home.

Syllogizing Sis Fuss

If all black
   men are liars, then
      all black men
         steal. If all black
        men steal then
           some black men are

still boys with toys
   and little heads and
      even smaller
         wrists handcuffed
           to one and the next. If one

  black man old big and stacked
    six feet tall up in a small room
       lacks provisions and can't
          find some thing of kind then

    we all hurt. And if we all
      hurt then we all hurt
         each other and the next.

Sis Fuss Goes Home

*The suspect is described as a
large black male in his 50's,
approximately 6' tall* On the outside
one was supposed
to be fine. Watch tv sleep
shit anytime. On the
outside *The robbery
occurred approximately
at 6pm near the
corner of Waterman and* the world would
shift and make sense
because always the
sun was always shining
outside and the women *according to
Sgt. Pitwick, the victim* the women
with smiles miles
long *is considered armed and
dangerous* waiting arms ready to rub a
head and trust and see a man and smile.

Sis Fuss Locked Back Up

        Dumb books
and too much
   ignorant attitude. Small
 space the press
     of loud men the smell
       of sit be still wait. And the only
   woman you know weeping
 on the other
    side of that plastic
       empty world. Old jokes
     stories that ain't never true.
  Time and day
 after day. But
home where that white rock
  could be placed
 high up on the shelf
hidden in the walls of the skin and
   the strings pulled
     tight made song.

Sis Fuss Epilogued

Sis lay on the bed cords
and calm and Kools his
sister's hand on his chest. No,
it wasn't his sister it
was Cassandra leaning

her elbow on the white stone.
She was watching him lashes
flitting in the sunlight
body in profile the laundry sign
behind her blinking gold. She

plucked a solo string a bit sad
scratched an old snake shaped scar.
And even though he could almost see the bars

behind her smell the spoiled water
in her big hair remit into a hard else
he choose to focus on her
hand tiny clawed her half crooked goofy

smile because damn it was such
a nice way to wake up.

About the Author

Nikia Chaney is a founding editor of shufpoetry, an online jour-nal for experimental poetry, and an associate editor for Inlandia: A Literary Journey, a journal for regional literature. She has been published or has publishings forthcoming in the Iowa Review, Saranac Review, 491, Pearl, Portland Review, and the New York Quarterly. Nikia's poetry has been chosen by Nikki Giovanni as the winner of the 2012 OSA Enizagam Poetry Award. Of her poem "the fish", Ms. Giovanni writes, "...What power this... song this friend sings for a friend drowning in if not evil, then certainly, difficulty." Nikia has been the recipient of grants from Cave Canem and the Barbara Demings Memorial Fund, and her book, *thump* was a finalist for the Marsh Hawk Press Poetry Prize. Her chapbook, *ladies please* is forthcoming in 2013 from Dancing Girls Press. She teaches English at San Bernardino Valley College along with local community workshops.